Mazurka

poems by

Katieann Vogel

Finishing Line Press
Georgetown, Kentucky

Mazurka

ACKNOWLEDGMENTS

Thank you to the *Monterey Poetry Review*, whose editors kindly published
"On the Path," "The Comet Summer," "Siskiyou Lullaby," "Asilomar," and
"The Wild House." Thank you to *Sokol San Francisco*, who published "Mezi
Duchy je kotvení," "Šťastný," and "Ocean Waits for You." Thank you Jevin,
Shara, Pacific University, family and friends for your support and guidance.

Publisher: Leah Huete de Maines
Editor: Christen Kincaid
Cover Art: Katieann Vogel
Author Photo: Katieann Vogel
Cover Design: Elizabeth Maines McCleavy

Order online: www.finishinglinepress.com
also available on amazon.com

Author inquiries and mail orders:
Finishing Line Press
PO Box 1626
Georgetown, Kentucky 40324
USA

Contents

OPENING NOTES

Prelude 3
She Calls My Name 4
Libu & Her Sisters 6

RIVER

Minneapolis River Round (Mazurka) 9
Hometown Girl 10
Fugue in River Minor 13
Big Frog Lake 14
Memory of Childhood 15
Valley Walk 16
The Den 17
Šťasný 18
Dream Home 19
I hope/ the forest leads me home. 20

OCEAN

Deepwater Spirit 23
The Wild House 24
Mezi duchy je kotvení 25
Asilomar 26
Otter House 27
The Comet Summer 28
Bahíahogar 29
On the Path 30
Ocean Waits for You 31

for Helen & Joan

Opening Notes

Prelude

after Judith Appleby

ENHEDUANNA, FIRST POET

FOUR HUMORS, HIPPOCRATES

LIBUŠE, FOUNDER OF PRAGUE

HOLY TRIUMVIRATE
POLYPHONIC MENSURAL
NOTATION

BOMBA DEVELOPS IN
PUERTO RICO

FLORENCE NIGHTINGALE
PROPOSES PRECURSOR TO
FIRST DIAGNOSTICS AND
STATISTICS MANUAL OF
MENTAL DISORDERS

PLENA DEVELOPS IN
PUERTO RICO

BABIČKA DANCES MAZURKA
IN CHICAGO

PROZAC INVENTED

NIETA SINGS
BY THE SEA

She Calls My Name
After Bob Kaufman's "The Poet"

Through the darkness, through the mist,
she finds me. In my most solitary hour,

> she wraps her arms around me.
> She is my cloak in winter.

Listen to this music she says
as churchbells ring and crickets sing
> in the field at sunset.

Come home when you are ready she says
> while the world tries to break me, while
I pick my heart up off the ground.

In front of me
there is a pit of bones
— *Creation* —

she tells me I am made of stone.

You can sit on this side,
you don't have to cross
she says softly while I cry

> and I know I have to cross
> and I have to cross it slow.

She sends sweet orange butterflies
to fly around and make me smile
while I climb down out of the sunlight.

Small figure stands there, dark in the distance,
> *smoke-orange sky surrounds her.*
> *I call to her,* Patience.

Her back straightens.

The pit is wide, I dance here in the cavern.
I can be myself here.
I don't mind crossing slow.

Libu
& Her Sisters

holds

Who

the

line.

rod &

fishing

the

of

Truth   is   the

worm

where

end

on

the

is

river?

the

River

Minneapolis River Round (Mazurka)

I see love   course   shiver
in the trees
      in the water

Cloaked in the green quilt
      my grandmother made for this family

Grandmother is God of this family
      Someday it will be my mother

Is she ready   Is she ready
      Am I ready to be

Little white-haired garden woman
      with her brown cat

Big things   Little things
      all flow out from this river

You could say I don't see everything
      But I am not just one woman

I have the eyes of every woman
      Her nose   Her mouth

We move like a waterfall

Can you feel us   course   shiver
      our bones in this river

Hometown Girl

Spirals, spinning, spyro-graphs,
tie-dye, soft serve, sculptures
in butter, Dairy Queen, meadow
princess, the Place I call home. Knots,

> pines. Lustrous lumber
> > education. Twelve-year-old
> > > mind. Come from

California, California
come Caribbean, before
that Bohemia, place of my mother's
> > mother's
> > > mother's

spirals set in motion.
Grandmother sips her tea.
Woman of rivers, woman of pines.

> > Father
> > > baker
> > Brother
> > > pilot
> > Cousin
> > > blacksmith.

> Her mother, taker-in
> of needy people. Her mother's mother…
> my mother…

> Maybe generations come in threes. The
> question, the answer, then me.

I am not from Minnesota. Homeless
by bloodshred design—
> certain insanity of the mind—
my blood

                    Boiled—
                              Ellis-ian passage un seen.
                    Trace elements of ocean in my blood remain: salt-en-
crusted veins.

          I am not from
Minnesota. But I want to be

like the three trees in the forest—passing associations. People
and people and people. People and people and
people. People before my people. Spirals,
lakes, and ancient rivers. Glaciers, lakes, and

dwindling time. Small white girl in large
green state::Purple state::that's me. Black brown white
obsessed with color   flowers in the meadow   I'm obsessed with
          obsessed with
obsessed with rhythm   whitegirl   obsessed with the clock   she's

black brown white white black brown obsessed with obsessed with
ob-

          Grandmother's home, burned.
          Some lessons are twisted in metal. Some lessons take
          centuries to learn.

Grandmother offers prayers for a new nation—
a flag with no stars—
          a flag, when you look at it, you know where you are.

A flag: bannered, black brown white purple green.

                    Bannered flag bandera waving
              Waving mariposa pulling
          Pulling pluscamperfecto high school
       High school education training
          Training aprender desaprender

Desaprender mi idioma porque
Porque nadie me dijo
Me dijo you are okay exactly
Exactly as you are.

What's that accent? Didn't catch it. Didn't
catch the inflection. You don't sound
like you're from California. You don't
look like you're from Puerto Rico. You
look Minnesotan. Now that's

who are you
who are you
who are you

who you are

Fugue in River Minor

Three skeletons stand watch

       at the bow of my bed. One
       plays accordion, the second

plays chimes. The third skeleton
holds the violin close to his chest,

       strumming sweet and grotesque

music drummed up from a world

       beyond my own. And the river courses—
       one, two, three—the man in my bed,

the skeletons, and me. We float
down the long, gaunt river, searching

       spirits infested with dreams.

Big Frog Lake

There is another world I visit
when I swallow the small pink pills. I don't think
the doctor knows I go to this place.

He asks me *How are you feeling?*
I sigh. It sounds like I'm sad, but
I'm also tired from visiting the other world.

I go there on my mountain bike. I ride
down Middle Road, off the pavement
and into the forest. I ride straight for Big Frog Lake.

I grind the bike pedals and I fly over the leafy hills.
I tell the doctor, *I don't like the way I'm feeling.*
He gives me more pink pills. And I fly

desperately, aggressively

                        I fly

quickly towards my death. At Big Frog Lake,

I lay down my bike and lift up my skirt and wade
into the water. There, things are cool and explicable
to my senses. I breathe deeply and dive

to the bottom. At the bottom it is very quiet.

My breasts bob in deepwater currents. No one
beckons me and no one looks away.
I can't tell the doctor about this place.

Memory of Childhood

a roadrunner in the backyard
under the balloons
      the rest is hard to remember

I heard a cry from the kitchen
as I huddled with *Exodus* in my bedroom

      out the window
      that giant bird and a spider
            plaintiffs before the mountain

stash the Bible
press face to window
feel vibrations of mother crying

      Mother
      crying in front of the cupboard
            looking for the sweet thing
      desperate for the sweet thing

balloons fly out from the mountain
red ones green ones gold ones
      the balloons I remember

      hot air jet spooks the roadrunner
            spider crawls in through the window
I hold her sweetly in my hands

      was my mother looking
      for the sweet thing in the cupboard

      how many pills does it take to find it

Valley Walk

There's a valley where all the wheels come off the trains
    I walk here every day

        hey hey
                I'm feeling crazier than usual today

I'm not sure I can walk it back
        and I'm not sure I want to

Doctor says, *Get some rest, take your pills and pray*

        hey hey hey
                I'm feeling crazier than usual today

At the top of the hill, there's an eye
        that sees through wind and rain

        Doctor says, *There are ways to manage the pain*

Choo choo
        I'd take the train
                but the wheels fall off

        hoot hoot
                owl flies by day

hey hey
        I want to walk it back   this valley's insane

        Doctor waves from the train

        hey hey hey
            hey hey

The Den

Last year I became aware
of foxes; now I see
them everywhere. Red

  foxes, spirit
                foxes, mountain
foxes. Carnal

        cuddly clever. I fear
              foxes. I need them too. When
              my stomach hurts—somedays

I am nauseated after eating—
I know something
inside of me is not
            right. *Help*

I ask the foxes. They come
to me in laughter. They ride
the wind of my breath

                    into my stomach. They curl

against my intestines. They walk
me to the garden. I pick a flower and eat it raw.
I see flowers everywhere.

Šťastný

Jeden medvěd,
   jedna liška,
   jedna žába,
jedna ryba,

      jedna babička.

Lucky Me

One bear, one fox,
   one frog,
one fish,

one grandmother.

Dream Home

We'll begin with the bathtub. Clawfoot diadem
on the porcelain-laden pate. Attic bathroom. A diving board
juts through the roof. Climb climb climb
up the chimney then dive through. The tub

is a twenty-foot tunnel (I hope you can swim)
that drains into a thousand-gallon aquarium
on the first floor. The davenport is submerged
for your underwater pleasure. Don't open
the front door. It takes ten hours
to refill the living room.

In the kitchen
you'll find
ten live owls
hooting in the freezer.
They're Ice Owls. Don't open
the freezer after sunset.

Are you hoping to start a family? Don't.

You'll find the neighborhood charming. This house
was built in 2082. Time travel won't be
available here until the 60s.
Internet is dial-up.

You'll see the backyard has the lovely orchid garden. Those will burn
each year in September. Plant basil in the spring. It activates
the soil and the giant orchid worms that live
under this lot. You'll need leashes to walk the worms in winter
(and a permit for basil-planting).

Here are the keys. Any questions?

I hope

        the forest leads me home.

I don't know how I'll look when I reach
    the other side. I don't know

        if I'll arrive in a sane place
    before I die. I am in
the season of change,

        on the cusp of understanding
        how a forest survives
    a winter freeze: how pine needles exhale

excess water; how the aspen ejects
    its leaves to withstand expected heavy snowfall
        and persistent frigid breeze. I know

    to face the surging winter, I must
be kind and bold and satisfied. I hope

    I get to keep those names when
I'm on the other side. I want
        to find the sunlit corridor
         where terror melts

    in springtime breeze. I hope

    to know myself enough someday to trust
this change with ease, to want a name

softer and stronger than an institutional disease.

Ocean

Deepwater Spirit

Now I am the moon. As light I move
through Santa Lucia peaks. I see in shuttered glances
the lovers in their white sheets. His hands

cup her breasts as she presses
herself against him. She exhales brute
steam from her lungs and heats

the window beside their bed,
porthole between worlds. Now the man
is an octopus. His tentacles reach for the pearl.

The woman is a rocky reef.
The eel finds her crevices. Deepwater
currents seep. The ocean moves—ink stains the sheets.

The ceiling collapses. There is a flood in the street. Dark
clouds push east.

I return to the mountains.
The lovers continue
to swim in the deep.

The Wild House

Asleep in the Wild House of wood and stone,
three types of beast dream: the woman, the cat, the ghost.

Together in the vision worlds, they coast
from realm to realm in cypress tree bark boats.

From the east, cool winds of black and green blow gently
in their pine-bough sails, and comet dust

showers the woman's hair in gold. Russet-
colored sparks shoot from the sleek-bodied tabby

cat's tail. The ghost plays the musical bow, a curio
from the time before the known. Sailing

softly westward, their six eyes see a gleam
on the horizon. Worlds collide before

them, great flashes send them tumbling, reeling
back to the barren world farthest from dreams.

Mezi duchy je kotvení

Andělíčku a mou dušičku,
    malé vlákna nás spojují.
I ve tmě je strážníčku:
    příze z příběhů babičky.

Mooring between Worlds

Little angels and my soul,
    small threads bind us.
Between worlds and lifetimes,
    this lifeline endures:

        yarn from grandmother's stories.

Asilomar

for J

The monarchs have mostly left, flown north
to cooler milkweed, but one still flies

here in the forest of evergreen
and hawk-watched live oak. The female

black widow spider crosses
the forest path, amber hourglass

tucked loosely on her abdomen.
White seagull cries then

lands softly in the cypress tree.
Fog bank builds over the water and disperses.

Beneath the cypress, a woman
kneels to watch the coyote, who watches

her, hazel hair over eyes soft
from late nights under the waxing moon.

Otter House

All the little otters
    floating in a row
don't care
      the rain is coming.

All the little otters
    playing in the sand
don't plan
      to build a castle.

All the little otters
    swimming in the sea
                hunger
    for life below.

All the little otters
    sleeping in their beds

—knock—

    they will let you in.

The Comet Summer

There, her longing, pulled taut
like crossbows fastened on the deer
who drinks from the high-summer stream—

sipping, not salacious, delicate,
white-tailed, flipping—there she dances
in the burgeoning sweetlight

of the comet summer's moon.
Deeper than her longing for time
beyond the August hour where

centipedes eat browning leaves, her hope grows
like blackberries in the thistle, drowned
in simple syrup, cocktail of clockticks. Deeper

than clocksand, a valley of shadows
and trances looms. Deeper than valleys,
one small flower blooms. Elemental

music sifts beneath the old-growth
vines. She dances. The clockbell
chimes. Deeper than August, a season

like a miracle appears. The bows slip—
the deer vaults the stream and lands
here—hooves of ironsoil glisten.

Bahíahogar

Where was I located the December before I was born? Did I exist
separately in my mother and father? Was I aware
my union was coming? I think my grandmother

　　called to me through the heavens. She was in her brick
　　house in Chicago, and she saw me with the angels. *Child,*
　　I'd like to meet you, she whispered to me in her dreams.

Or was it my grandfather in his New York
house of stone? Did he see me buried under
the earth, churning with fire of 10,000 years? Did he reach

　　　　his left hand, which was part spirit,
　　　　into the Old Ghost River, and touch
　　　　my fine hair flowing in the electric currents

of hell? Perhaps it was my own soul's volition
that brought me to this island mated between sea

　　　and sea and sea.　　Maybe

　　I was a wave in the ocean, or a sip of wind, or the tail
　　of a green sea turtle, or the eye
　　of a humpback whale.　　　　Maybe

I smelled the arroz con frijoles
wafting through wooden gates
along the adoquines, and I could not wait

　　　one more minute
　　　to float this earth
　　　with two human feet.

On the Path

The pressure to reveal yourself
disappears in faces
of ocean waves, slapped back
into foam into sky

into bird's wing, hyper-tense and apathetic.
Brief reprieve from atrocity, white foam washes
brown rock. In ten thousand years everything
crumbles. Today pelicans dive

over otter heads, dolphin spouts, seal suns
past the breakers. The tidepool is a mirror:

you are wind, shadow. Deeper below water: solid rock
shimmers, magma core to radiant surface.

Ocean Waits for You

Don't settle, don't settle
little oyster in the bay. One day

the wind will pluck you
by the shell and place you
on the hearth. You'll boil

until the necessary grit
sticks to your pearlish heart.

Katieann Vogel's writing and art have appeared in numerous publications, including the *Monterey Poetry Review, Sokol San Francisco*, and the *Children and Nature Network*. She works in her Monterey, California community as a writer, artist, and outdoor educator. Katieann was a 2024 Maritime Research Fellow at Mystic Seaport's Munson Institute, and she is a graduate of Pacific University's MFA program, where she was a Katherine Dunn Scholar. She and her partner enjoy fishing and hiking along the coast. In her poems, Katieann honors her grandmothers, the ocean, and changing tides.